How To Draw
DOGS

Written and Illustrated by **Carrie A. Snyder**

Watermill Press

Introduction & Materials

Drawing is a skill that grows with practice. You can train your eyes, hand, and mind to work together, and this book will show you how this can be done. When drawing dogs, spend time observing your own pet, or those of neighbors and friends. It's always a good idea to carry a sketch pad around with you. Of course, it's difficult to get a dog to pose for you. But you *can* make quick motion sketches, and draw the details later. Study the shapes of the eyes, nose, ears, and paws of your subject. Fur direction and length are also important. Remember that practice is the key to becoming a good artist. It's a lot of fun to draw, so take your time as you work and enjoy!

The materials shown below can be used for the drawings in this book. Pencils are the best medium for a beginning artist. The softness or hardness of the lead produces different textures. The softest pencil is a No. 6B. This pencil will give you soft tones. A No. 2 pencil has harder lead, which gives sharper detail lines. A black drawing pencil is especially good for drawing dark dogs, such as the Doberman pinscher. A medium charcoal pencil also gives a soft effect. A kneaded eraser is important to have. This type of eraser won't leave any crumbs on your artwork. You can also shape it and pick out highlights with it. After your pencil drawing is finished, spray it with a fixative. This will keep it from smearing.

Pen and ink, as well as felt-tip markers, are harder to work with than pencils. Once you draw an ink line you can't erase it as you can a pencil line. This is why it is important to first sketch your guidelines in pencil. Then you can tell if the body structure is correct before going to your final drawing. The pencil guidelines can be erased later. Each medium has a charm of its own, so choose the one you like best for each dog.

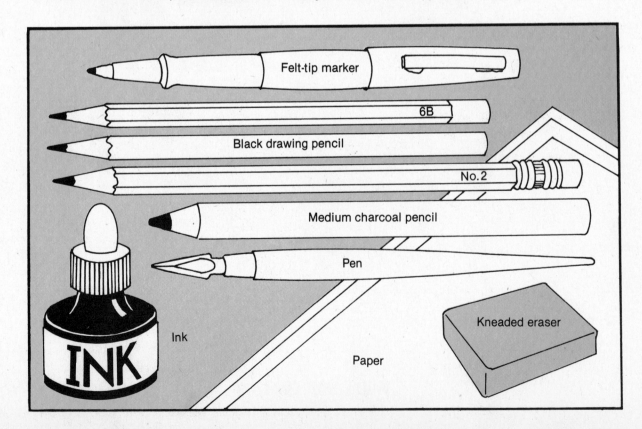

Felt-tip marker

6B

Black drawing pencil

No. 2

Medium charcoal pencil

Pen

Ink

Kneaded eraser

Paper

Basic Shapes

Always begin your drawing with the three basic body masses: the head, chest, and hindquarters. Use a soft pencil to draw these forms. If you have to correct something, just erase it and start again. The sizes and shapes of the body masses will vary according to the breed of dog you're drawing, but they will always be there.

Draw the muzzle and add the neck lines. After this, connect the chest and hindquarters with the back and stomach lines.

Now draw the guidelines for the legs and paws. Add the ear, tail, and eye. Once you are happy with this basic outline, you can start drawing the details.

A No. 2 pencil was used for the final sketch. The side of the point was used for the shaded areas, and the tip of the point for the details.

Head

Chest

Hindquarters

Heads

When drawing the head of any dog, always remember these three basic shapes: the *circle* for the top of the head, the *cone* for the muzzle, and the *cylinder* for the neck. No matter what angle the head is at, these shapes will always be present. After your basic outline is finished, you're ready to draw the eyes, ears, nose, and mouth.

Circle (Head)

Cone (Muzzle)

Cylinder (Neck)

Three-quarter front view of German shepherd

Side view of pointer

Front view of German shepherd

Springer spaniel

Bloodhound

Siberian husky

5

Features

You should take some time to study each dog's characteristics, and practice drawing the more difficult features, like the eyes, ears, nose, and paws. The eyes are the most expressive part of a dog's face, and by putting in small highlights, you can make the eyes sparkle. A highlighted area will also make a dog's nose look shiny and wet. In time, you'll be able to identify a breed of dog just by looking at its ears. When this happens, you'll know that all your observations and practice have paid off. And your drawings will show it!

Paws

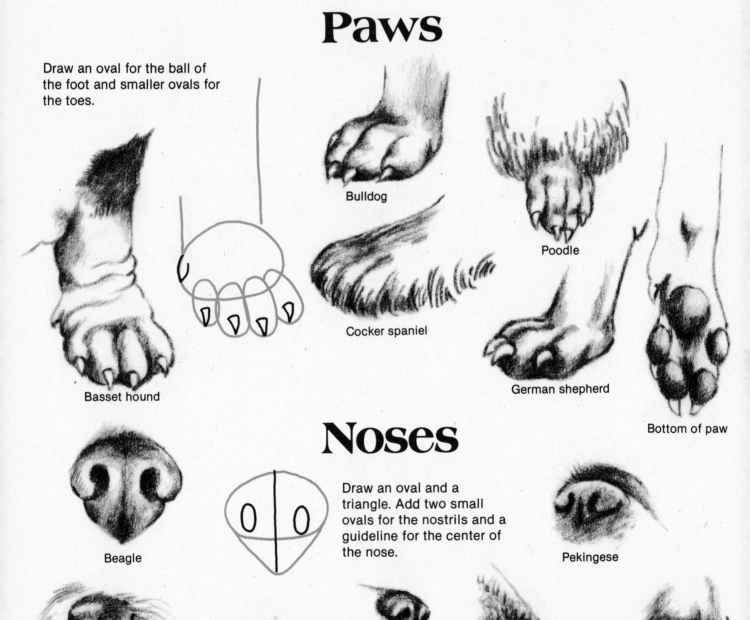

Draw an oval for the ball of the foot and smaller ovals for the toes.

Bulldog

Poodle

Cocker spaniel

German shepherd

Basset hound

Bottom of paw

Noses

Draw an oval and a triangle. Add two small ovals for the nostrils and a guideline for the center of the nose.

Beagle

Pekingese

Poodle

Dachshund

German shepherd

Bulldog

Basset hound

Ears

When drawing the ears of any breed of dog, always look for the "cup" shape.

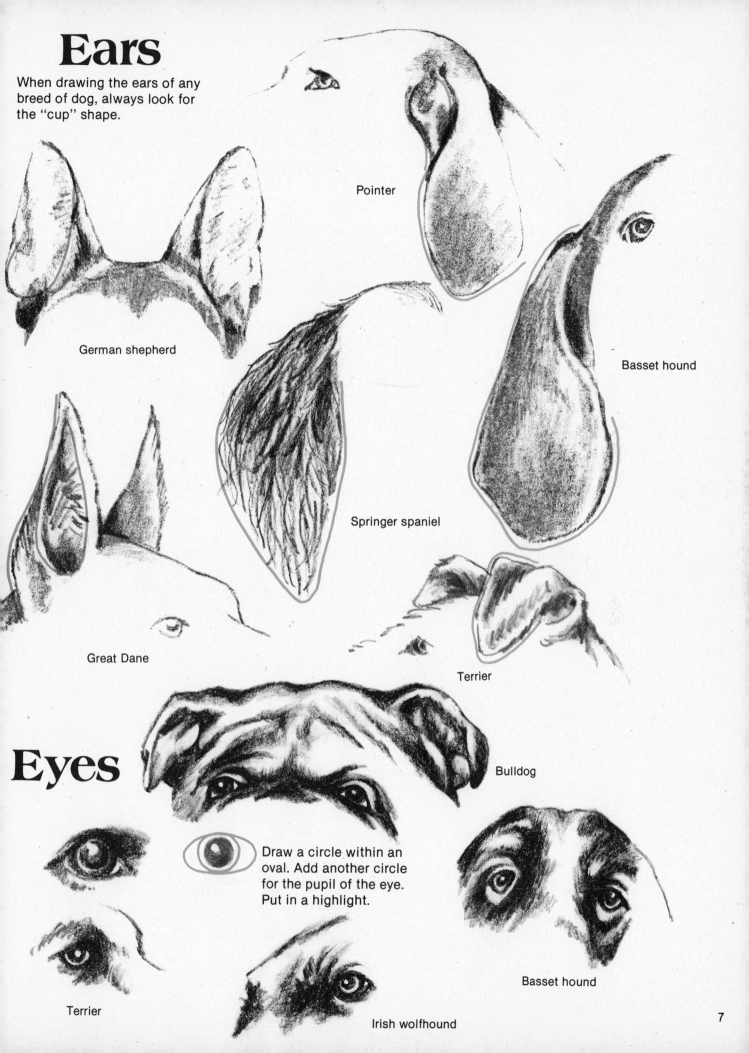

Pointer

German shepherd

Basset hound

Springer spaniel

Great Dane

Terrier

Bulldog

Eyes

Draw a circle within an oval. Add another circle for the pupil of the eye. Put in a highlight.

Basset hound

Terrier

Irish wolfhound

Dachshund

The name *dachshund* is German and means "badger-dog." This dog's ancestors fought the fierce badger. With its long body and short legs, the dachshund could easily fit in the tunnels of the badger's underground den. The dachshund's coat can be smooth, wire-haired, or long-haired.

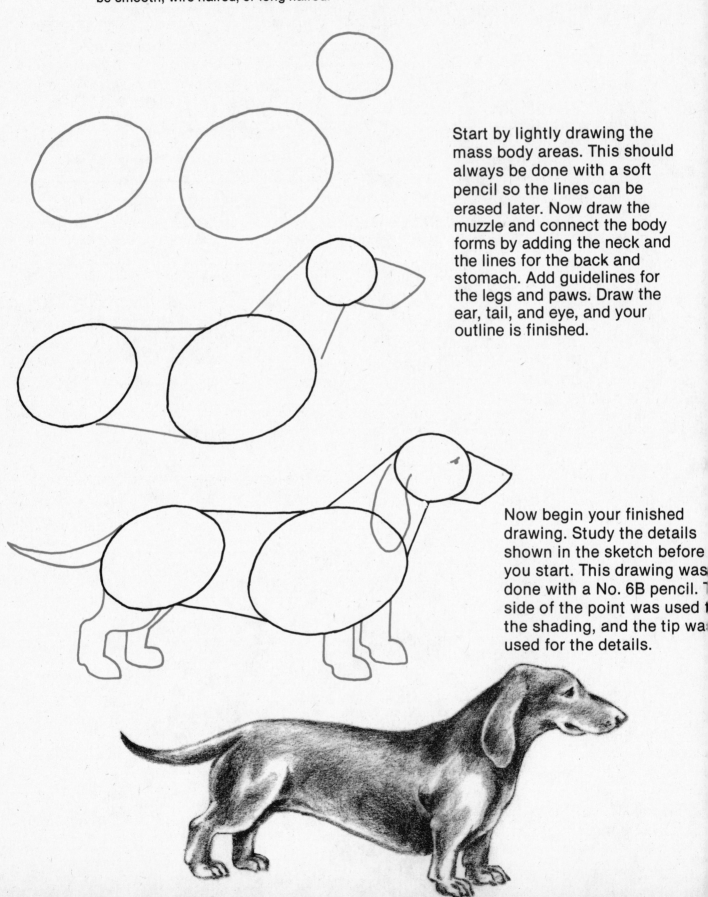

Start by lightly drawing the mass body areas. This should always be done with a soft pencil so the lines can be erased later. Now draw the muzzle and connect the body forms by adding the neck and the lines for the back and stomach. Add guidelines for the legs and paws. Draw the ear, tail, and eye, and your outline is finished.

Now begin your finished drawing. Study the details shown in the sketch before you start. This drawing was done with a No. 6B pencil. side of the point was used the shading, and the tip wa used for the details.

8

Golden Retriever

The golden retriever is a cross between the Russian tracker and the bloodhound. In 1860, the British developed the breed, making it smaller and increasing its scenting powers.

Lightly sketch the mass body areas with a pencil. Start with the head, chest, and hindquarters. Add the neck, back, and stomach lines. Then add the muzzle, eye, and ear. Draw the guidelines for the legs, paws, and tail. Study the finished drawing before you start drawing the details.

This drawing was done with a medium charcoal pencil. Use the side of the point for the shading.

Boston Terrier

This breed is often called the "American Gentleman." The Boston terrier is a combination of the English bulldog and the English terrier, and was first bred in Boston. The Boston terrier seldom gets into fights and has a very gentle disposition.

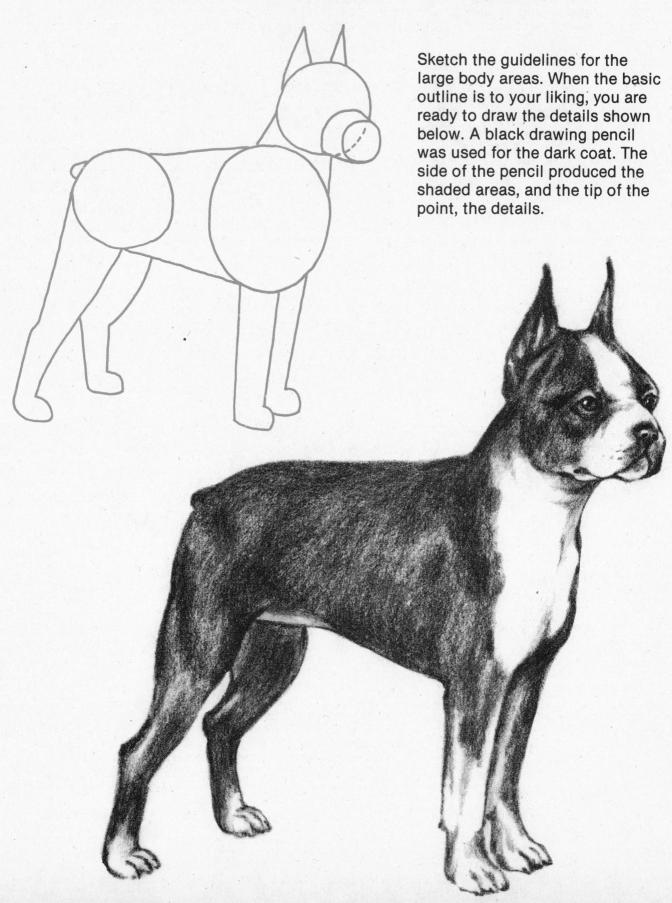

Sketch the guidelines for the large body areas. When the basic outline is to your liking, you are ready to draw the details shown below. A black drawing pencil was used for the dark coat. The side of the pencil produced the shaded areas, and the tip of the point, the details.

Poodle

The poodle is the national dog of France. There are three varieties: the standard (average height, 20 inches or 50 centimeters); the miniature (average height, 12 inches or 30 centimeters); and the toy (average height, 8 inches or 20 centimeters). There is also a larger miniature called the *moyen caniche.* The poodle is a descendant of the German Pudel. Poodles are very good hunters and retrievers.

Sketch the outline forms with a pencil. Remember that the poodle drawn here is well groomed, and its fur is very fluffy and soft. A No. 6B pencil was used. The side of the point will give you the shading, and the point will give you the details. Study the drawing below before you start your final drawing.

Miniature poodle with a Dutch clip.

German Shepherd

The German shepherd was used in Germany as a herding and farm dog. This breed is often called the "police dog." The German shepherd was used during World War II for many important assignments. It is also used as a guide dog. This breed of dog has a double coat—a dense undercoat and a harsh overcoat.

Draw the mass body areas. Start with the head, chest, and hindquarters. Add the muzzle, ears, eye, and tail. Draw the lines for the neck, back, and stomach. Now add the legs and paws. When the outline seems right, you can start drawing the details.

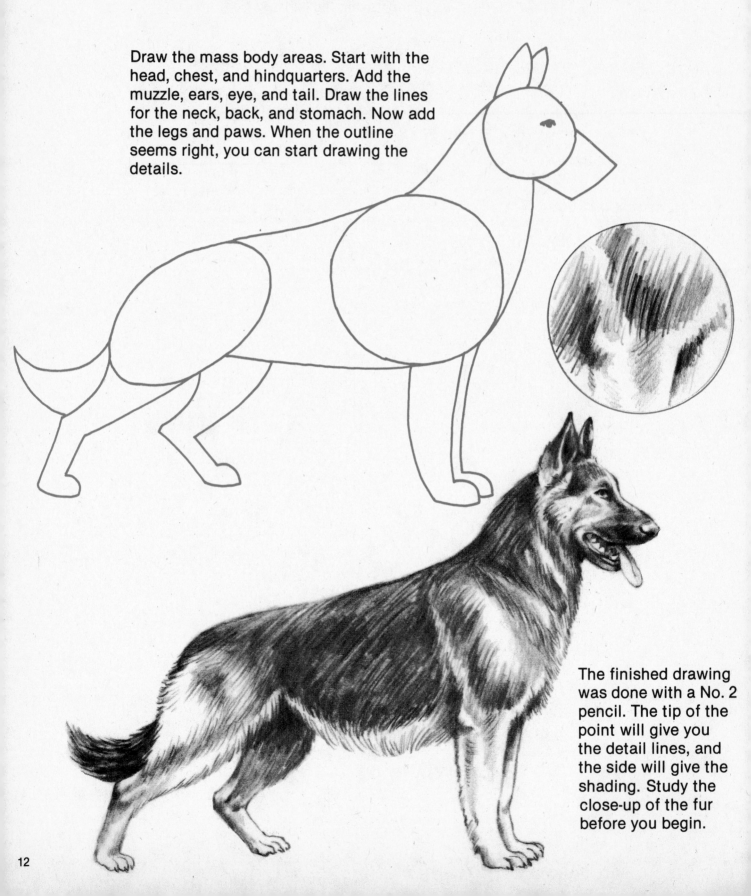

The finished drawing was done with a No. 2 pencil. The tip of the point will give you the detail lines, and the side will give the shading. Study the close-up of the fur before you begin.

Dalmatian

The Dalmatian is one of the oldest breeds of dogs. This breed existed many years ago in Dalmatia, a former province of Austria. The Dalmatian is best known as a firehouse dog and carriage dog. Its spotted coat is short and sleek.

Lightly sketch the mass body areas with a pencil. The drawing below was done with a felt-tip pen. Study the details of the dog before you start to draw them.

Schnauzer

The schnauzer originated in Germany in the fifteenth century. It is a combination of the black poodle, wolf-gray spitz, and the old German pinscher. This breed comes in three varieties: the miniature (average height, 12 inches or 30 centimeters); the standard (average height, 20 inches or 50 centimeters); and the giant (average height, 25 inches or 63 centimeters). The schnauzer's coat has a wiry texture.

The dog shown here is a miniature schnauzer. Start by drawing the mass body areas. This should be done lightly with a pencil, so it can be erased later. When you are happy with this outline, start to draw the details shown in the finished sketch. This drawing was done with a No. 6B pencil. The side of the pencil was used for the shaded areas, and the tip of the point produced the details. Study the close-up before doing your final drawing.

Scottish Terrier

The Scottish terrier, or Scottie, originated in Scotland. It was first used to hunt rats and other small animals by the Highlanders. The Scottie has a thick wiry coat, which is usually black, and sometimes gray, sandy-colored, or white.

Draw the basic outline with a pencil. This breed is very short and stocky. When you have finished the outline, study the close-up of the fur. Now you are ready to start drawing the details. A felt-tip pen was used for this drawing.

The Scottie is usually black. To draw the thick, dark fur, you'll have to draw many overlapping strokes. Parts of the body should be solid black.

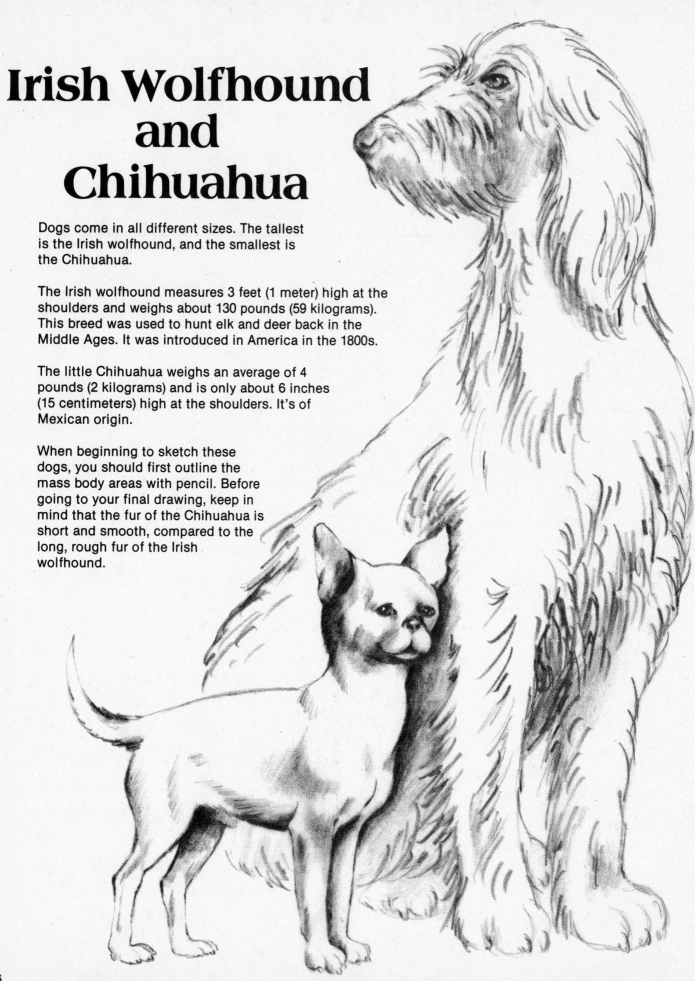

Irish Wolfhound and Chihuahua

Dogs come in all different sizes. The tallest is the Irish wolfhound, and the smallest is the Chihuahua.

The Irish wolfhound measures 3 feet (1 meter) high at the shoulders and weighs about 130 pounds (59 kilograms). This breed was used to hunt elk and deer back in the Middle Ages. It was introduced in America in the 1800s.

The little Chihuahua weighs an average of 4 pounds (2 kilograms) and is only about 6 inches (15 centimeters) high at the shoulders. It's of Mexican origin.

When beginning to sketch these dogs, you should first outline the mass body areas with pencil. Before going to your final drawing, keep in mind that the fur of the Chihuahua is short and smooth, compared to the long, rough fur of the Irish wolfhound.

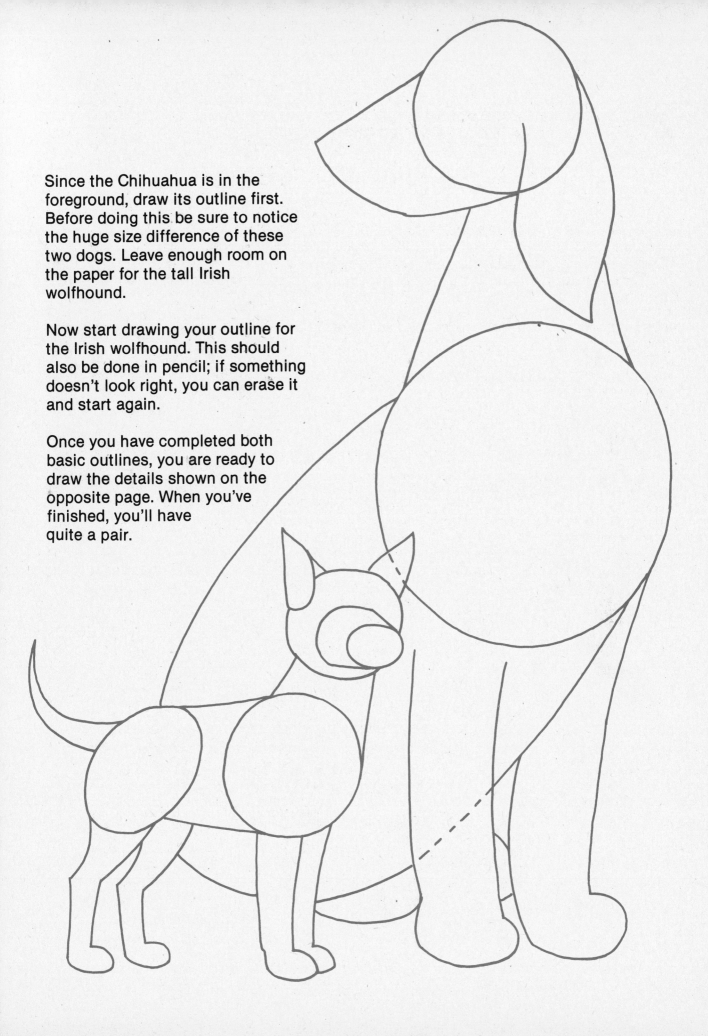

Since the Chihuahua is in the foreground, draw its outline first. Before doing this be sure to notice the huge size difference of these two dogs. Leave enough room on the paper for the tall Irish wolfhound.

Now start drawing your outline for the Irish wolfhound. This should also be done in pencil; if something doesn't look right, you can erase it and start again.

Once you have completed both basic outlines, you are ready to draw the details shown on the opposite page. When you've finished, you'll have quite a pair.

Samoyed

The Samoyed was originally brought from Iran to Siberia by nomads. In Siberia, this dog pulled sledges and guarded herds of deer. The Samoyed is an Arctic animal and does its best work in snow and ice. Its thick white coat protects it from the freezing Arctic temperatures.

Lightly draw a pencil outline of the basic body areas. Notice the sweeping lines used for the curl of the tail. The Samoyed has a lot of thick fur, especially around the neck area. After you have completed the outline, study the finished pen and ink drawing below and start drawing the details. It would also help to study the close-up shown below.

Because the Samoyed is white, you'll need fewer lines than you would on darker breeds of dogs. These lines show the shading and texture of the fur.

Beagle

The beagle, the smallest of the hounds, is one of the oldest breeds known. This dog runs very quickly, which makes it a good hunter of rabbits and hares. The beagle has a short coat, which may be white, black, and different shades of brown.

Draw the basic outline in pencil. When you are satisfied with this you can go on to your finished sketch. A No. 2 pencil was used for this drawing. Study the close-up shown below for the technique used. Remember that the beagle has a short coat that is fairly smooth.

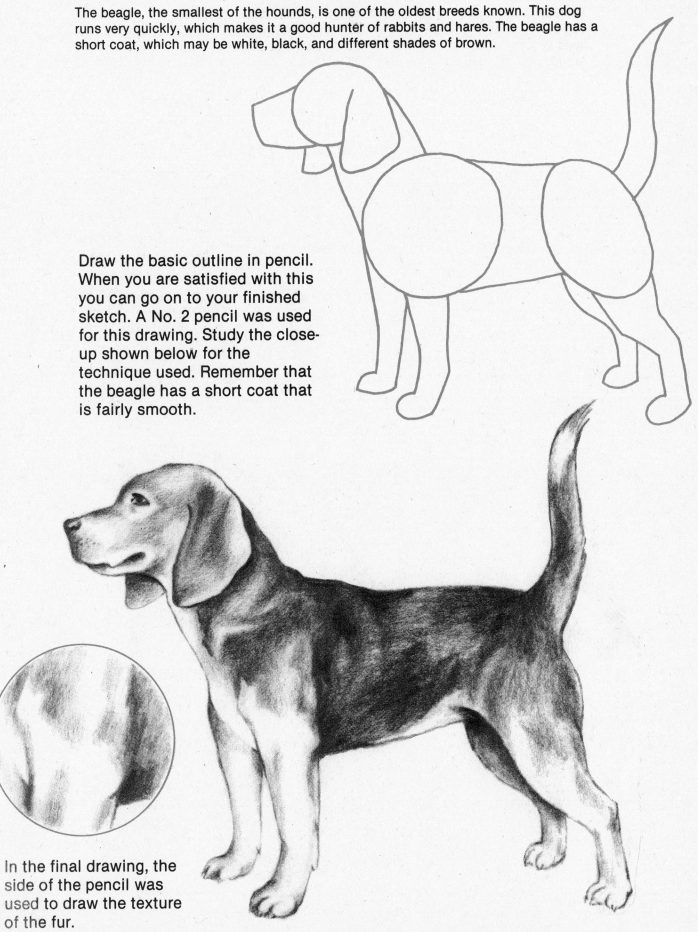

In the final drawing, the side of the pencil was used to draw the texture of the fur.

Old English Sheepdog

As you might have guessed by its name, the sheepdog originated in England. It's known for its rolling, bearlike gait. The coat is long and full. The English sheepdog comes in shades of gray and black, with or without white markings.

Draw your guidelines in pencil. Make the outline any size you want your drawing to be. This finished drawing was done with a No. 2 pencil. The side of the pencil produced the shaded areas, and the point was used for the details.

Cocker Spaniel

The cockers are divided into three groups: solid black, any solid color, and the spotted cocker. The cocker spaniel has a very wavy coat. This affectionate dog is easily trained and makes a good pet.

Begin your sketch the usual way, by drawing the mass body areas lightly with a pencil. When you're satisfied with this outline, you can begin to add shading and details.

Since the cocker drawn here is black, a No. 6B pencil was used. By using the side of this pencil, you can draw the shading needed to show the thick fur. The tip of the pencil will give you the details. Study the close-up before you start.

Bulldog

The bulldog is Great Britain's national dog, as well as the mascot of the British Navy. This breed was used to bait bulls and bears in the 1600s. Today, the bulldog is considered to be a very gentle dog and makes a good pet for children. Its short coat may be red, grayish, white, or mottled.

Lightly sketch the body areas with pencil. The bulldog is quite stocky. Keep this in mind when drawing your outline. A black drawing pencil was used for the finished drawing. The side of the pencil gives you the dark patches as well as the shading of the smooth fur. The point will give the details. This breed has many wrinkles on its worried-looking face.

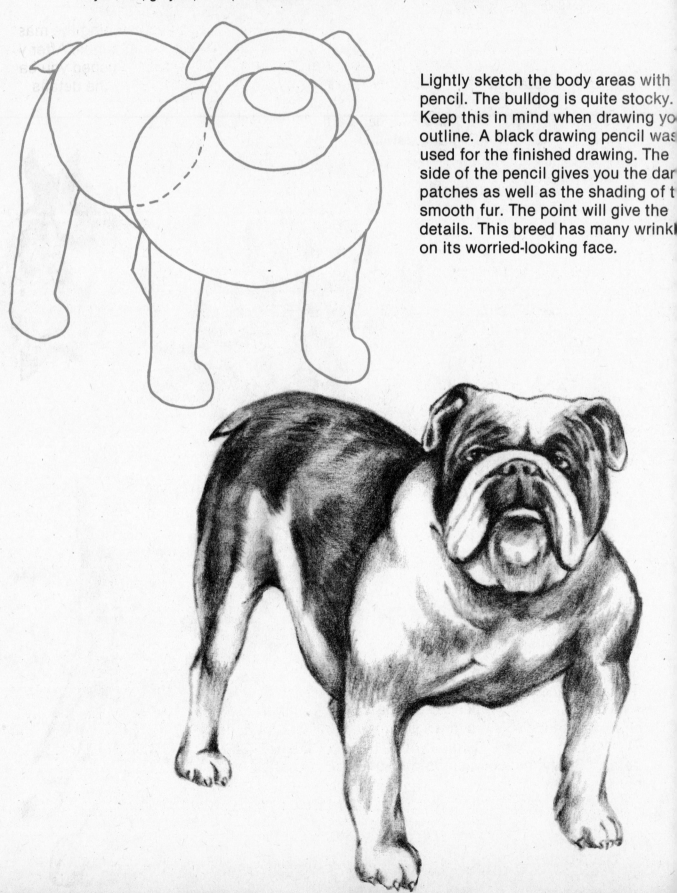

Boxer

The boxer originated in Germany. The name comes from the way this dog uses its paws when playing. This breed became popular in the U.S. in the 1930s. The boxer has a short, smooth coat.

Start by sketching the mass body areas with a pencil. After you get the outline finished you can begin to draw the details shown below.

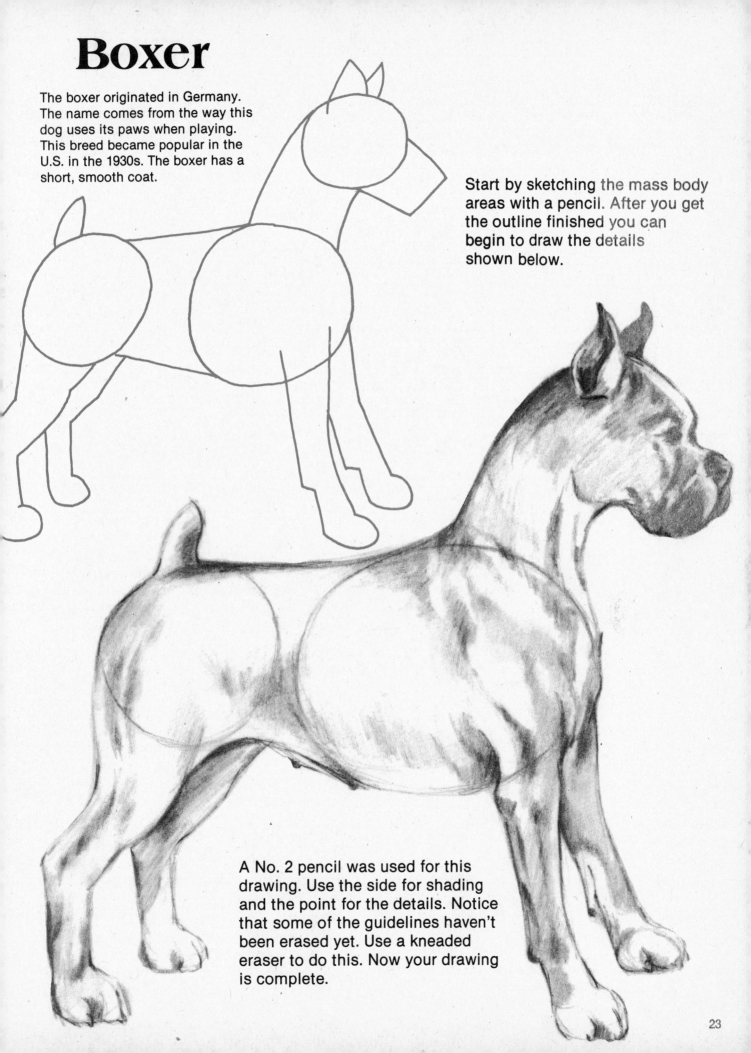

A No. 2 pencil was used for this drawing. Use the side for shading and the point for the details. Notice that some of the guidelines haven't been erased yet. Use a kneaded eraser to do this. Now your drawing is complete.

Wire-Haired Fox Terrier

There are two varieties of the fox terrier. One type has a smooth coat. The one shown here has a thick, wiry coat. This terrier was used as a hunting dog in England. Its coat may be white with black or tan markings, or both.

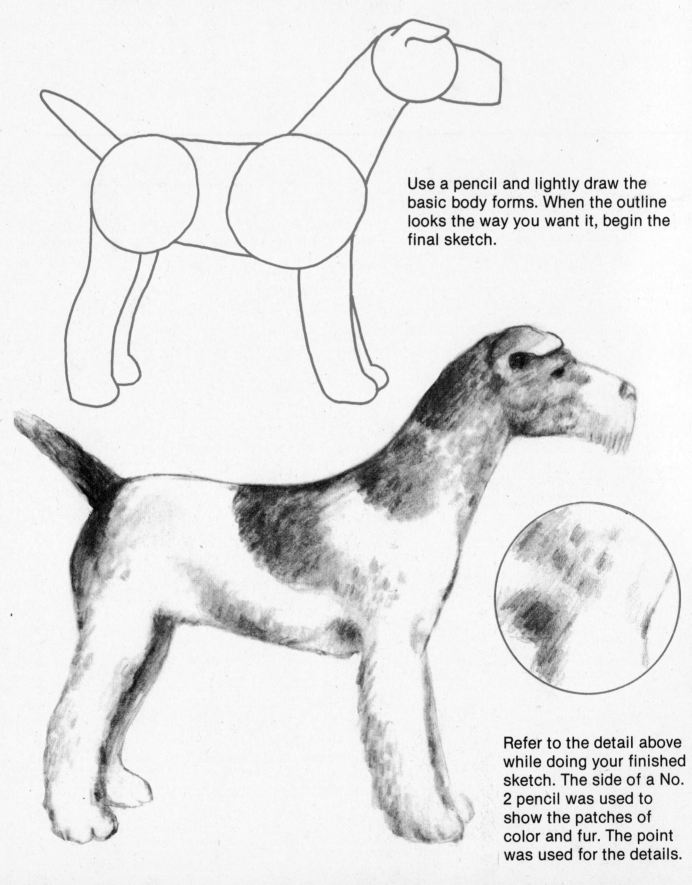

Use a pencil and lightly draw the basic body forms. When the outline looks the way you want it, begin the final sketch.

Refer to the detail above while doing your finished sketch. The side of a No. 2 pencil was used to show the patches of color and fur. The point was used for the details.

Basset Hound

The basset hound originated in France. It's a cross between the French bloodhound and the St. Hubert hound. The early French kings used the basset hound to trail deer and other game.

Start your drawing with the mass body areas. Once you are satisfied with this basic outline, you are ready to begin your final sketch of this sad-looking, but lovable hound.

This sketch was done with a No. 2 pencil. The basset hound has smooth, short fur. The texture of this fur can best be drawn by using the side of the pencil. For the details, use the tip of the point.

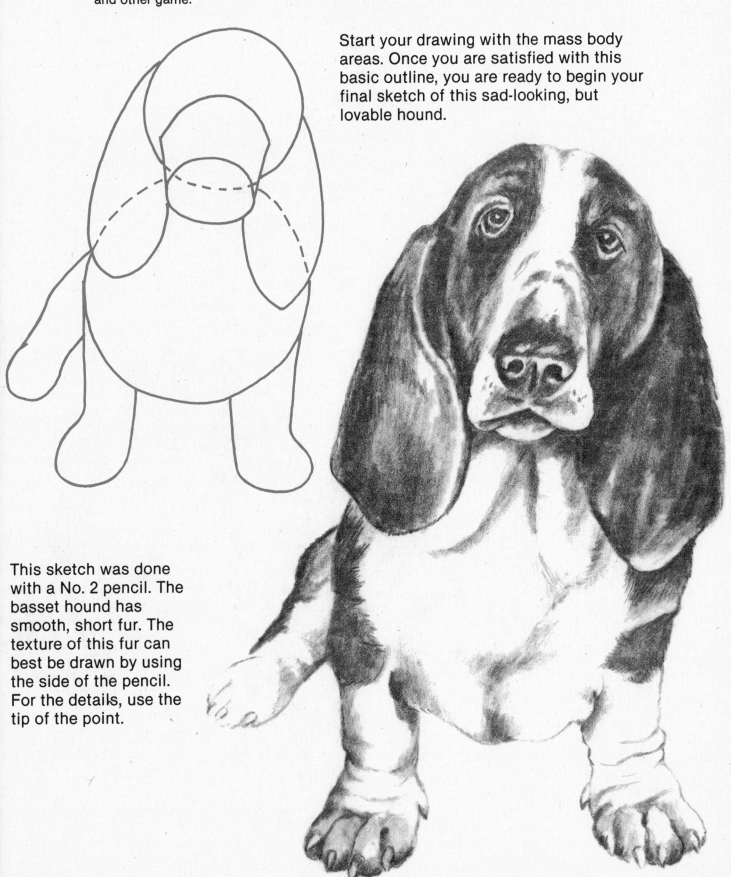

Doberman Pinscher

The Doberman pinscher originated in Germany, and is named after the famous dog breeder, Louis Dobermann. This breed is a combination of the old short-haired shepherd, the black and tan terrier, and the smooth-haired German pinscher. It's best known as a guard dog and police dog.

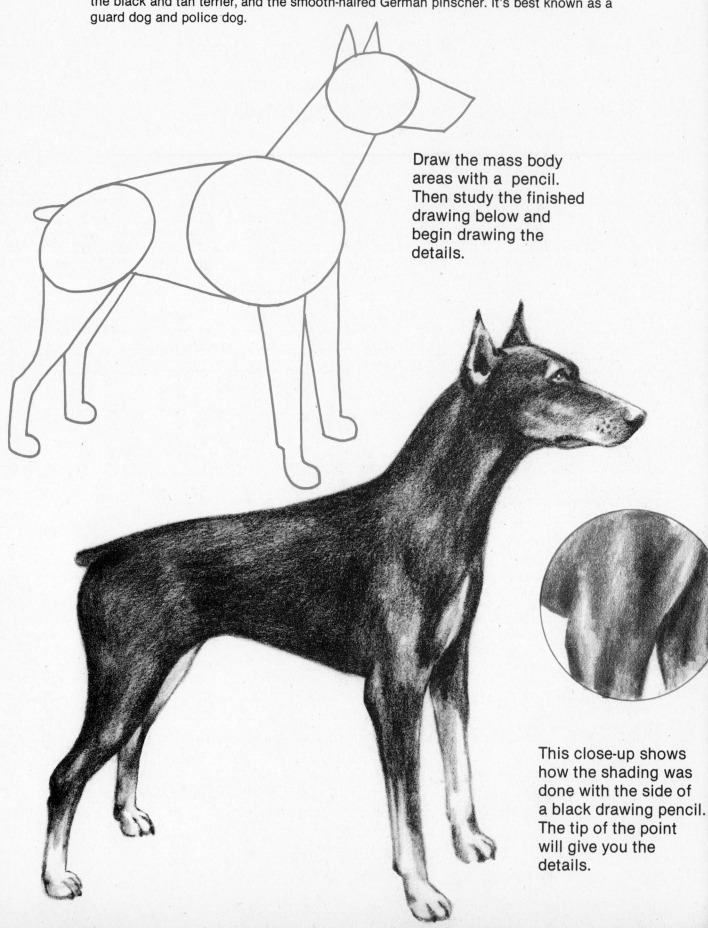

Draw the mass body areas with a pencil. Then study the finished drawing below and begin drawing the details.

This close-up shows how the shading was done with the side of a black drawing pencil. The tip of the point will give you the details.

Cairn Terrier

The Cairn is the working terrier of Scotland. This dog got its name from the piles of rocks called *cairns,* where it was constantly burrowing after game, such as rats, otters, and foxes. This breed has a thick, rough outercoat and a soft undercoat.

The Cairn is a short and stocky dog, as most of the Scottish terriers are. Keep this in mind when drawing your pencil outline. After completing the outline, you are ready to start drawing the details. Study the close-up of the technique used for the finished drawing.

A No. 2 pencil was used. The tip of the point will give the details, and the side of the pencil will give the shading.

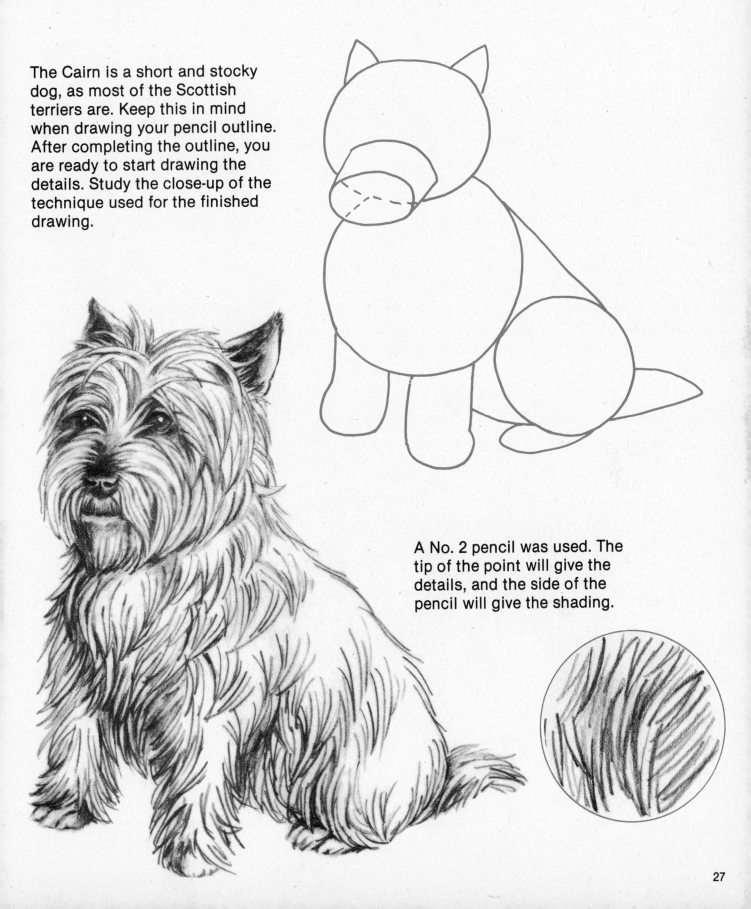

Collie

The origin of the collie traces back to Scotland around 1700. There it was used to herd sheep. Queen Victoria of England popularized the breed in 1860. The collie's coat has long, soft fur.

Sketch the mass body areas in pencil. The muzzle is long and pointed. When you've finished your basic outline, you can start drawing the details shown below. First study the close-up.

This sketch was done with a No. 2 pencil. Use the side for shading and the tip for details.

Pekingese

The Pekingese is an ancient breed of dog from China. It dates back to the Tang dynasty, and at one time, this dog was considered to be sacred. Although it doesn't look the part, the Pekingese was used as a hunting dog. Its fur is soft and wavy.

Draw the mass body areas with a pencil. Now draw the guidelines for the face. Don't leave out the tongue. Once this is to your liking, you can start your finished drawing. There are two techniques shown for this dog. Choose the one you like best, or better yet, do them both. If you use a No. 2 pencil, remember that the side of the point will give you the shaded areas.

Pen and ink

No. 2 pencil

The Pekingese makes a good subject for a pen-and-ink drawing. The shading is produced by adding more ink strokes.

Afghan

The Afghan hound was pictured on ro[ck]
carvings in Afghanistan over 4,000 yea[rs]
ago. This type of dog was then taken [to]
Egypt, where it was bred by nobles. Th[ey]
called the Afghan the "monkey-faced"
hound. The Afghan has great speed a[nd]
can jump over very high obstacles.

To begin your sketch, lightly draw[n]
the mass body areas with a penci[l].
Remember, if there is a part of th[e]
outline that doesn't look right, jus[t]
erase it and draw it again. Once y[ou]
have finished, you are ready to ad[d]
the details shown below.

This sketch was done with a No. 2
pencil. Use the side of the point to
draw the shading, and the tip of the
point for the details.

Great Dane

This breed, which originated in Germany over 400 years ago, was used to hunt wild boar. Because of its size, the Great Dane is referred to as the "King of Dogs." This dog got its name from the French, who called it *grand Danois,* which means "big Dane." Its average weight is 130 pounds (59 kilograms).

Note the long torso and legs of this breed. Start by lightly drawing the mass body forms. When this is done, you can start drawing the details. A charcoal pencil was used. The side of the point will give the shaded areas.

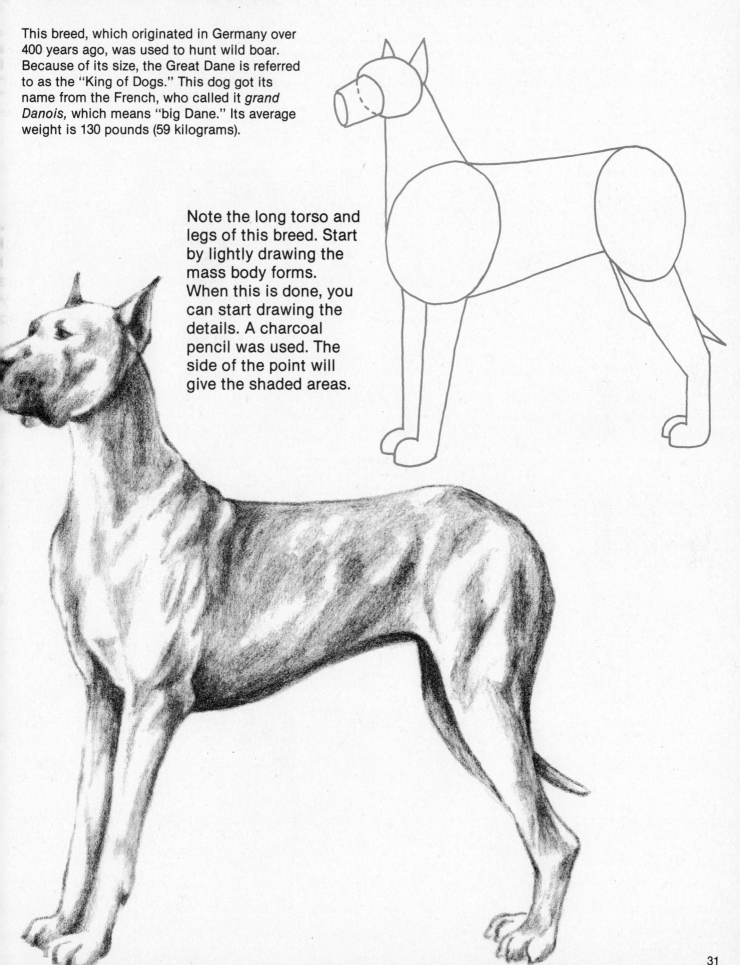

Mixed Breed

The mixed breed, or mongrel, can be a cross between two breeds, or a combination of several breeds. This dog can be any size, shape, and color. It might have the nose of a basset hound and the tail of an Afghan. Any combination is possible. With its own special looks and characteristics, each mongrel is a one-of-a-kind dog. These dogs make great pets. They have a lot of love to give.

Draw your pencil outline first. Remember the cone, circle, and cylinder forms of the head and neck. Add the ears. Now draw the details.

Lightly draw the mass body forms with a pen When the outline is finished, add the detai shown below.

This drawing was done with a No. 2 pencil. Use the tip the point to get the details, and the sid for the shaded are